OASIS
Rest Awhile

PHYLLIS B. PARUN

Copyright © 2022 PHYLLIS B. PARUN

All Rights Reserved. No part of this publication may be reproduced or transmitted in any means, electronic or mechanical, including photocopying, recording, or any information storage and retrieval system, without permission in writing. For permissions contact the author.

Permission to make copies of any part of this work can be submitted in email to pbpstudio@yahoo.com

Cover art and all illustrations are solely owned by the author and require permissions.

Botello Bronze Chairs in San Juan
Cover Photograph and Design by Phyllis Parun

ISBN: 978-1-7323560-7-8

BERNARD PRESS
Publisher

New Orleans, Louisiana

First Edition

DEDICATION

In memory of
all my generous talented teachers

CONTENTS
Author Selected

I - <u>New Orleans Born</u> *excerpts*

II - <u>New Orleans Between Poetry and the Blues</u> *excerpts*

III – <u>My Dance with Time</u> *excerpt*s

IV - The Hurricane Ida Journal

V - Haiku Notebooks

"An artist's duty is to not leave this life as a barren wasteland."

Atasaro Migumori
(19th Century Japanese poet and artist)

I

I

New Orleans Born
Excerpts

WORSHIP

This is my church
This poem.
It is she where I worship
And she who worships me
There is none other.

It is the solemn word
The poignant phrase
The unseen, unspoken beauty
That I worship.
The poem, my altar
The prayer to life, my deity.

That is my church
Where I worship -
None other.

~

Oh, beautiful moment
Precious illusion
> *Do not flee!*

APRÈS DÉLUGE

So often I long for home -
for the old New Orleans   -
my New Orleans,
that New Orleans I was born into
that I grew up in,
the New Orleans of my heart
now in my memories

And even though it is all   -   still here
the past and the present
the living and the dead
the fantasy and the reality
side by side.
Still I long for home
as if it wasn't.

THE POET'S CAT

Sleeping 'til dawn
The poet's cat
Has no visible means of support
Her only work remains
   the cleaning of her claws
   and the eating of
   uncountable nibbles
   then begging for more
   mostly for attention
   rather than from hunger.

She is the well-fed pet of the poet
   lying around all day at the foot
   of the immobile writer
Who leaves her chair only
   to change chairs
While the only sound the cat hears
   is the scratching
   of the pen on paper
   or the spoon clank on
   the food bowl.

The poet's cat runs
   up and down the house
   her paws pounding noisily
   on the wooden floorT
then sitting patiently on the rug
   designated for brushing her
   she waits for the scratching
   of the pen to stop
sometimes amusing herself with
any piece of string she can find.

The poet's cat is kind
The poet's cat is vigilant
   patiently waiting every morning
   for the Sun to rise
   for the candles to go out
   for the poet to tire
of the company of words
and be amused by her.

~

DOORS

Unafraid, they leave their doors -
unlocked
These artists who live in
   wooden houses
   filled with books and paper,
   pens and paintbrushes.
What do these mean to a thief
   these tools of the creative,
   these materials which
   give form to ideas?
They cannot be resold
Their value is not monetary -
Nothing there can be stolen.

Unlocked and unafraid
   their doors open
   their souls unarmored
   vulnerable to the world
These creative ones leave traces
    of where they have been.

II

II

New Orleans Between Poetry and the Blues
Excerpts

A visit with old friends
At the Museum
Works of art.

~

TEARS

Red eyes
Cheeks wet with tears
   I am forgetting you.

~

DECADES

Decades go by and
years come back
first, as a spot on the distant
horizon
then moving full figured into
view memories from that
deep within
placed there long ago
when we were young
and innocent
of life's inevitabilities

~

III

III

My Dance with Time *(2022)*
Excerpts

Grandfather opened an upholstery and furniture repair shop in the front of their cottage. Grandfather and Grandmother Wolters had three daughters, Marie Philippine the oldest, Sophie Ada the middle girl and the youngest, Dorothea Catherine, my mother. As children, the three sisters, worked in the Wolters family shop, each developing different trade skills.

    Broken chair seats
    Worn furniture
       Nimble fingers

It was 1962. The Vietnam War was on. As my younger brother turned 17, the draft threatened. Our Retired Army Major Father knew from experience what it took to survive war. He knew soldiers and that his son wasn't a fighter, commenting, "he would surely be killed." Deeply concerned, he set about to find a way to save his son from battle.

Off the front room of our home on Gentilly Boulevard, was a closet which Father had made into a small office by putting in a long narrow desk just big enough for a couple of pads of paper. That day he entered his office, pen in hand and closed the door, emerging several hours later with a fist of papers. Calling his son over, he announced that my brother should join the U.S. Air Force, which would just be entering the war four years later, the very year my brother would be discharged, thus avoiding both draft and battle.

My brother did just that and it turned out exactly that way. Father's World War II experience served him well. Stationed in Virginia for a year then on the Aleutian Islands for the remaining three years, my brother had avoided war.

    Happy father
    Happy brother - both
      Alive

When my Father died I inherited his book collection as my brother had little interest in any book that wasn't a chess book. Father's library was small, consisting of less than 50 books, unlike my enormous 3,000-book research library. How different we were in this regard. Of course, all of Father's were read and reread and very potent ones they were too: sports, games, philosophy of life, poetry, instructional manuals, personal conduct - while there are books in my library with spines yet to be cracked.

>When he died
>Time stopped - later
>>*It started again*

Father's most cherished book was a small black notebook of inspirational quotes. Its contents were sometimes handwritten while others were clippings from newspapers meticulously glued onto black pages. Father carried this book with him throughout World War II from 1942 through to 1947, from First Lieutenant to Major in Kobe, Japan. This was his personal bible - these poets and writers - his priests.

    Recreation athlete
    Army Major - poetry
      His bridge

As inspiration, on my 16th birthday, my parents gave me the first edition of Janson's <u>The Picture History of Painting</u>. That was the beginning of classical art and my many aesthetic love affairs.

    First art book
    Michelangelo's women
        Half male

When I bought a Nikkormat in 1976, the pictures I snapped were just bout every subject.. Photography was like framing a beautiful scene. Thinking back on my experience, I realize that my first photographic mentor was my Aunt Sophie, our family photo-documentalist. When Aunt Sophie departed this life at the grand old age of 94, she left behind a legacy of 2,000 slides and photographs and 20 reels of 8mm and Super 8 film with one simple message: "time passes so take the picture".

> All things perish
> Beauty lingers
> *Forever longing*

There were few departments. Philosophy was one of them. When Dr. Daniel Anderson, a PhD. Graduate from Tulane University, accepted the appointment as Chairman of the new Philosophy Department, he selected twelve students from the freshmen class. I was one of them – why, I have no idea, as I was no academic. However, it may have been because I showed some youthful propensity for argument that he saw as trainable. I had, after all, inherited the fine art of questioning authority and being a contrarian from my immigrant military-gamesman father who loved the French art of repartee and verbal sparing. .

    That pile of books
    Unread thus far
       In living

Andy, as he was known to his students, was a teacher of philosophy and also a master of puns. It was not uncommon for him to run puns for 20 minutes while his students appropriately hissed, booed and yawned. Each student had our favorite form of humor. Droll humor and tongue-in-cheek became my favorites along with occasional well-placed sarcastic wit.

Whereas sarcasm can be readily recognized in a written text, tongue-in-cheek rarely can, as it is invisible, and an author's private chuckle which sneaks up on the unsuspecting reader, even educated ones, catching them unaware.

So dear reader beware, I carry on in his honor with glee!

    Pining
    For old pals
       The past is present

A few months later Andy died. That telephone call was my bon voyage, his deathbed retort personifying the supremacy of his Socratic method. Like his venerated predecessor, Andy had died of the quintessential Western philosopher's disease. But then perhaps he was right after all, there is no such thing as too much thinking.

    Ask a question
    Get an answer
       Yet another question

After graduating, it was my good fortune to be admitted as a graduate student to the Department of Philosophy at the University of Pennsylvania. There were few females in the field of professional philosophy worldwide then which is still true today sixty years later. So for a southern female philosophy student in the USA to be accepted into an Ivy League university was a worthy prize and validation of academic achievement.

With very few female philosophers in the sexist patriarchal university system, I was never able to get a university teaching position because of the subjugation of educated women. Publishing my own writing was the only way I could get heard. We were not wanted. Ruth Bader Ginsberg born five years earlier that I experienced the same doors closing in her face, as did every educated woman of our post WWII generation. Barred from university professorships, law firms, and discriminated against in hiring women were told we were either too qualified or not qualified enough.

Out of the womb
Full strident women
Hammered by patriarchy
Standing tall
   Out living them

Remembering what Dr. Anderson has told me, "You may not be able to get a post at a university to teach, but your education has prepared you to think clearly and logically. That is by far a greater achievement, indeed."

Decades passed, three of them, I still felt that western philosophy was fundamentally deeply flawed but I had been unable to identify what those flaws were through the application of western logic alone, a fruitless circular endeavor indeed. It was Ludwig Wittgenstein who had placed the final nail in the coffin of Platonism calling all philosophical questions "nonsense" - and nonsense it all seemed.

The philosophy of the Orient had been lost to the west around 340AD with the burning of the Alexandra Library. Only fragments of what came before Plato had survived in the basement. Thinking of these early manuscripts as insignificant, centuries of western university philosophers minimized their contributions labeling them "Pre-Socratics" as if nothing existing before Plato held any academic merit. Nonetheless, even these fragments led to discoveries.

   East West North South
   Four dimensions
      Looking for truth

So I turned to the Orient.

IV

IV

The Hurricane Ida (2021) Journal

Aug. 29, 2021
On the 16 anniversary of the devastating floor of 2005, hurricane Ida blew in.

Aug. 31 - Day 1 Monday

Ida came to town
Leaving me with
Shingles flying off the roof
Rain coming into my study
And me awake in the night emptying
buckets of water
No ATT landline on this first day
After the insolent hussy left town.

Sun setting now
Darkness descending
The cicadas sing their happy song
Candle lit in the drawing room
Open French shutters.
A little cool breeze flows
I hear my mother, her sisters and my brother
Talking, laughing, and playing games
All the way back to my early childhood
I finally feel at home.

Sept. 4 – Day 6 Saturday

Downriver power has returned
Come 16 blocks up river
Please

9/5/21 - Day 7 Sunday

August 29
Katrina and Ida
Two unwelcome sisters

9/6/21 – Day 8 Monday

1
Ida took
Mother's family house
Leaving weepy eyelids behind

2
One day too soon, the power will return
Piercing star studded peaceful nights
With noisy civilization

3
When the power when out, there was a daily emergency radio broadcast which I listened to each day. To conserve batteries I used a small double A battery radio listening for any information about Red Cross locations for ice and water, Fema information, any warnings, operating filling stations and any city and government instructions. One day this news slipped in.

    Cardinal Burke said COVID was an anti-   Christ Wuhan agenda
    Then he contracted COVID
    He was right, after all!

9/8/21 – Day 10 Wednesday

Two days later Tuesday listening in the
dark the emergency broadcast
reported a disturbance forming
off the coast of Mexico.

    Bay of Campeche
    Waving at us
    Not - waving back

*

Since Ida stormed through
No COVID news for 12 days
What a relief!

9/9/21—Day 11 Thursday

Twelve days of Ida
In 95 degree heat with no power
No – not Christmas

*

News reported that Ida left the south and blew into New York.

    Hurricane disaster living
    Where should I move –
    Oh, I know - NYC
    Take a subway-boat to work

9.20.2021 – Day 21

Hurricanes, fires, earthquakes, viruses
Tears
Nature crying out

v

V
Haiku Notebooks
Excerpts

Haiku
few words
    aha

precious moment
beautiful illusion
    do not flee

no tears
grief oozes out
    in art

maturity
rear view
vision

born female
more brother than sister
the two of us

to live and die in Paris, a complete life
to live and dies in New Orleans
fate

family bonds
like sisters   yet
    more

far off into life I went
far far away
    from the ordinary

a child no longer
elder hood ahead
    success

a brief visit to childhood
cannot stay long
  being called forward

this house
of many shapes
  the sculptor's friend

footsteps ahead
too big to fill
  beware

youth
blessings and sorrows
    could not see ahead

exquisite moments
this one that one
    a haiku

born female
more brother than sister
    the two of us

chasing civilization
lined with carcasses
 serious misdirection

power outage
listen! the silence of nature –
 seldom heard in the city

leaves fall from the trees
verse slips from the pen
 it's autumn

fly lights on prose
slips on "so"
      washes feet

sounds of nature
sounds of the world
      rude collision

first times
memories of them
      no repeats

companion on the road
how far will you come
      before turning off

pandemic mask up quarantine
human herd stampede
      stilled

The artist's plight
having only mere words,
a pen, brushes, paper, canvass
on which to record all the lives
lived and witnessed -
such feeble imitations
      these tools seem

With limited lifespan
émigrés, all – from previous civilizations
dysfunctional nations,
displaced migrants,
slaves to wages
pioneers in some distant,
unimaginable future
carrying poisoned food and toxic water,
loving still - this
precious murdered, Earth

~

I've lived many lives in this one –
What's next
    Repeat please

PHYLLIS PARUN
Poet - Author

Phyllis Parun is a deeply honest author and a quintessential example of Cocteau's dictum that *"writing should be an act of love otherwise its nothing but handwriting."*

Born in the mysterious city of New Orleans, Parun is a self-styled creative with an individual intelligence whose voyage of self-discovery destined her to develop first as a visual artist then as a gilding craftswoman and a pioneer community *culture*r finally as philosophical poet. As a writer she has explored many literary forms: non-fiction, essays on healthy life, short stories, philosophical and poetic memoir. Community activism set her course of involvement in black, gay and women's rights and in the arts of the 1970s then in the healing arts of the 1980s-90s. This is an author who writes with insight and honesty about the human condition as she has experienced it.

New Orleans Born her poetic homage to her childhood family influencers and her city of New Orleans while **New Orleans Between Poetry and the Blues** continues to the year 2000 sometimes with scathing humor. **My Dance With Time** features stories from seven decades about the people, eras, and circumstances that shaped her life, inspiring personal tales which will take the reader on a deep journey this and reflection of their own long forgotten memories.

Ms. Parun's published genres include interviews, articles, essays, poems, e-Zines, visual art, and photography in a wide variety of local and national publications. The Beachcomber (LSUNO, 1961-63), AOBTA Pulse (2006), American Assn. of Oriental Medicine (1995), Macrobiotics Today (1991-2015), Gulf Coast Arts Review (2004), ArtLit (2006), Iris (2005), Qi: Journal of Traditional Eastern Health and Fitness (1995), The New Laurel Review (2001- 2015), The Maple Leaf Rag III (2006), <u>Mending for Memory</u> (2017) and creator of "The New Orleans Living Treasurers Award" and her self published eZine: "The New Orleans Avant-Garde" (2008 ongoing).

End Notes

Thank you for reading

**Sign up for
author newsletter and
new releases**

pbpstudio@yahoo.com

Published Titles

New Orleans Born (2019)
***New Orleans Between Poetry
and the Blues (2019)***
Love's Arrows (an EBook)
My Dance with Time (2022)

Order direct from
www.PHYLLISPARUN.com
"BOOKS FOR SALE"

Also available at
Your local bookstores,
Barnes & Noble,
Kobe, Amazon Kindle,
Goodreads, Walmart
Ingram Spark

REVIEWS WELCOMED
On Kindle at
Amazon USA
https://www.amazon.com/-
/e/B006HX9348

F i N

Notes

Notes

Notes

Notes

Notess

www.ingramcontent.com/pod-product-compliance
Lightning Source LLC
Chambersburg PA
CBHW071250070526
44583CB00017B/2413